EXPLORING THE SCIENCE OF NATURE

The Nature and Science of
AUTUMN

Jane Burton and Kim Taylor

Gareth Stevens Publishing
MILWAUKEE

For a free color catalog describing Gareth Stevens Publishing's list of high-quality books and multimedia programs, call 1-800-542-2595 (USA) or 1-800-461-9120 (Canada). Gareth Stevens Publishing's Fax: (414) 225-0377.

Library of Congress Cataloging-in-Publication Data

Burton, Jane.
The nature and science of autumn / by Jane Burton and Kim Taylor.
p. cm. — (Exploring the science of nature)
Includes bibliographical references and index.
Summary: Explains why the season of autumn happens and how it manifests itself in the weather and changes in plants and animals.
ISBN 0-8368-2190-4 (lib. bdg.)
1. Autumn—Juvenile literature. [1. Autumn.] I. Taylor, Kim.
II. Title. III. Series: Burton, Jane.
Exploring the science of nature.
QB637.7.B87   1999
508.2—dc21   99-21153

First published in North America in 1999 by
Gareth Stevens Publishing
1555 North RiverCenter Drive, Suite 201
Milwaukee, Wisconsin 53212 USA

This U.S. edition © 1999 by Gareth Stevens, Inc. Created with original © 1999 by White Cottage Children's Books. Text © 1999 by Kim Taylor. Photographs © 1999 by Jane Burton, Kim Taylor, and Mark Taylor. The photograph on page 25 (below) is by Jan Taylor. Conceived, designed, and produced by White Cottage Children's Books, 29 Lancaster Park, Richmond, Surrey TW10 6AB, England. Additional end matter © 1999 by Gareth Stevens, Inc.

The rights of Jane Burton and Kim Taylor to be identified as the authors of this work have been asserted by them in accordance with the Copyright, Design and Patents Act 1988. Educational consultant, Jane Weaver; scientific adviser, Dr. Jan Taylor.

Printed in the United States of America

1 2 3 4 5 6 7 8 9 03 02 01 00 99

Contents

Words that appear in the glossary are printed in **boldface** type the first time they occur in the text.

Top: Rose hips turn red in autumn and show that they are ripe.

Our planet travels around the Sun in a huge circle, called an **orbit**. It takes a year for Earth to complete one orbit. As it travels through space, over 1.6 million miles (2.5 million kilometers) a day, our planet spins on an **axis**, like a spinning top. The top is not upright. The axis leans at an angle of 23 degrees.

As Earth travels around the Sun, its north pole leans toward the Sun. Six months later, it leans away from the Sun. The tilt of Earth's axis causes the seasons. The seasons continue to change year after year because the tilt of Earth's axis never varies as it circles the Sun.

During autumn, Earth passes a position in its orbit where the Sun is directly over the Equator. During this time, days and nights, everywhere in the world, are each twelve hours long.

On September 22 or 23 each year, the Sun is directly over the Equator. This time of year is called the autumnal **equinox** in the Northern **Hemisphere**. During autumn, the days gradually become shorter. In the Southern Hemisphere, September 22 or 23 is the spring equinox, and the days gradually grow longer.

Near the Equator, there is very little change in **day length** throughout the year.

Above: An autumn day dawns pink at Grand Teton National Park in the Rocky Mountains of Wyoming.

Opposite: On an autumn day, roe deer have already grown their thick winter coats.

Below: After the Sun sets, autumn nights in the Arizona desert are cold and clear.

Autumn Colors

Autumn is a time of change. One of the most apparent signs of autumn in the countryside is the change in color. The green of summer gives way to the yellow, red, and brown of autumn. These are the colors of dying and dead leaves.

The leaves of some maples and oaks turn brilliant red. Aspen and birch leaves change to bright yellow before they fall. Beech leaves turn a rich golden brown.

Trees are **perennial** plants. Trees and certain other plants grow year after year and sprout new leaves every spring. **Annual** plants live just one year. Their leaves rarely turn bright colors in autumn. Leaves of annual plants change from green to muddy brown when the plants die after a frost.

Below: Leaves of the perennial plants bracken and thimbleberry turn yellow in autumn.

Below: Vine maples glow brilliant red in autumn.

6

Above: The round leaves of aspens turn delicate shades of yellow in autumn.

Above: Autumnal beeches in Europe turn a rich golden brown.

Most leaves are green because of the green pigment called chlorophyll that is in their cells. Chlorophyll is broken down and stored in a perennial over winter, while other pigments become visible in a brilliant presentation of color. When annual plants die, the chlorophyll is destroyed along with other pigments. The leaves wither, become brown, and fall. This is the end of the life cycle for an annual.

Below: In autumn, the leaves of many kinds of trees fall. They form multi-colored drifts together on the ground.

Below: Bull banksia has green leaves throughout the year. As new leaves grow, the old ones turn brown and drop off.

7

Seeds and Berries

Above: The seed heads of old man's beard look very similar to dandelion seed heads.

Below: Dandelion seeds are like little parachutes. They blow away in the wind to grow into new dandelion plants.

In autumn, many plants produce fruits. These fruits contain seeds. Fruits and seeds contain energy, often in the form of sugar and oil. This energy originally came from the Sun. Plants collect sunlight with their leaves and use the energy to make sugar, oil, and other substances. The Sun is strongest in summer, allowing fruits and seeds to grow. They are fully formed and ripen by the time autumn arrives.

The purpose of seeds is to grow into new plants. At the heart of each seed are **genes**. These are very complicated **molecules** that hold all the information a seed needs in order to grow into a new plant.

Inside a dandelion seed, for instance, the genes tell the seed to grow into a new dandelion plant. The seed heads of old man's beard look like

8

Left: Seeds of the horse chestnut are large and shiny. They fall to the ground in autumn. Squirrels and rats often carry them off and bury them.

Above and below: Squirrels cannot eat all of the nuts that a tree produces. In autumn, they bury many of the nuts in the ground. Nuts that survive the winter may start to grow in spring.

dandelion seed heads. The genes inside these seeds, however, make sure that the seeds grow into old man's beard — not dandelions.

Many of the seeds that plants produce in autumn will not start to grow immediately. If they did, the tender young plants would soon be killed by the cold of winter.

Many seeds have "devices" that prevent them from growing until winter passes. For instance, many tree seeds will not start to grow until after the seeds have experienced very cold temperatures.

Above: The fruits of the prickly pear cactus turn red to advertise that they are ripe and ready to eat.

Below: Rose hips are fruits that contain many seeds. Animals eat the fruit and scatter the seeds.

Some plants produce fruits that are juicy. The fruits taste good to birds and other animals, but the seeds inside are often bitter or are inside hard shells. Therefore, they serve no purpose to the animals. Animals distribute these seeds in various places when they discard them.

Small fruits called berries are specially designed for birds to eat. They are often brightly colored, and birds can see them from a distance. Berries change color from green in spring and summer to yellow, red, or black in autumn. In this way, birds know which fruits are ripe. Often, berries become soft and sweet only when they are ripe. Hard, unripe berries taste sour. This is the plant's way of preventing its fruits from being eaten before the seeds are ready.

When a bird eats a berry, the seed or seeds inside it are not digested. Instead, if the seeds are small, they pass straight through the bird. Large seeds remain in the bird's stomach until the fruit around them has been digested. The bird then brings up the seed, which falls to the ground and may later grow into a new plant.

Some trees and bushes carry a heavy crop of berries in autumn. Berry-eating birds rely on this food source to get them through winter. If it is a good year for berries, birds are able to survive the winter in that area. If there are few berries, birds will have a difficult winter.

Above: The green berries of holly start to turn red in early autumn.

Below: In late autumn, holly berries are a brilliant red. Birds, like this redwing, can see them from a distance.

Spore Bearers

Top: Lichens grow on tree trunks, rocks, and on the ground. Like fungi, they are spread by spores.

Above: Spore capsules are grouped on the undersides of a male fern's leaves. Numerous little cups in each capsule contain the spores.

Right: Hair moss spore capsules grow on the top of thin stems. When the capsules are ripe, their lids come off and the spores spill out.

Flowering plants produce seeds that can grow into new plants. **Flowerless plants** produce **spores** instead of seeds. Spores are very tiny. They blow in the wind and are carried in splashes of rainwater. Flowerless plants grew on Earth long before flowers appeared. These early plants shed spores by the millions.

Ferns produce spores in **capsules** located on the undersides of their leaves. When the spores become ripe, which is generally during autumn, the capsules open. Spores tumble out into the breeze. The spore capsules on mosses are separate from the leaves. These capsules grow on stalks above the leafy part of the plant.

Left: Mold spores float in the air everywhere. When one drifts onto an over-ripe tomato, it quickly grows into a forest of little knobbed stalks. Each knob contains thousands more spores.

Below: A boletus fungus produces millions of spores in the tiny tubes on its underside. When the fungus is growing, the spore tubes are vertical so that the spores fall straight down into the air below.

Many **species** of fungi produce spores in autumn. Their **fruiting bodies**, called mushrooms or toadstools, grow in the woods and fields during the damp autumn months. The fruiting bodies produce spores. Each mushroom or toadstool may produce a million or more spores.

When the fruiting bodies die, the fungus lives on as fine threads, called **mycelia**. They grow below the ground or inside rotting logs. The mycelium of one fungus may cover hundreds of square miles (kilometers) and live a long time. It can produce hundreds of fruiting bodies and billions of spores each autumn.

Autumn Storms

Top: A raindrop drips from cotoneaster berries.

Below: Autumn storms send huge waves crashing against cliffs. The waves cause rock to fall, and land is lost to the sea.

In some parts of the world, autumn is a time of high winds. The land and, particularly, the sea have been warmed by the heat of summer. They are at their hottest by autumn. This warmth causes water to **evaporate** and air to rise. At their most dramatic, these conditions can cause a huge, circular storm.

In the western Atlantic, this type of storm is called a hurricane. Exactly the same type of storm in the Pacific is called a typhoon. In the Indian Ocean, the storm is a cyclone. Typhoons are the biggest and most damaging storms on Earth because they form over the vast Pacific Ocean.

Left: Hurricane-force winds sometimes uproot even huge trees, such as this beech.

Below: Lightning often flashes from one part of a cloud to another without coming to the ground.

Autumn storms most often take the form of strong winds and heavy rains, without the damaging effects of a hurricane. However, water **vapor** and air movements in the atmosphere can give rise to another type of storm, known as a thunderstorm. Electricity can be stored in clouds, which are themselves made up of millions of tiny droplets of water. The droplets in a cloud become charged with electricity as they swirl around.

Each droplet carries a tiny positive or negative charge on its outside. If the droplets in one part of a cloud are all positively charged while the droplets in another part are all negatively charged, electricity may jump from one part of the cloud to another. This jump is visible as a flash of lightning. Sometimes, the ground itself carries the opposite charge to a cloud, and then the lightning forks down to the ground.

Mist and Fog

The sea holds warmth longer than land. The sea in autumn is still warm from the summer Sun, while the land is already starting to cool. Warm seas cause water to evaporate. As this moist air sweeps over the cold land, it cools. This causes fog to form.

Fog is actually just a cloud at ground level. It is made up of millions of tiny droplets. These form because cold air cannot carry as much water vapor as warm air. As moist air cools, the vapor in it **condenses** into droplets. Fog forms over the sea as well as over land. This happens when wind blows moist air from a warm part of the ocean over a cold part. This is why fog often forms around icebergs.

Mist is just thin fog. Mist often forms on windless nights. It lies in the bottom of valleys. The process that causes mist actually starts on the hilltops around valleys. There, on cloudless nights, warmth radiates from the ground, and the air next to it rapidly cools. Because the cold air is heavier than the warm air, the cold air pours down the sides of the valleys and lies at the bottom. If the air is moist, the vapor in it condenses, and mist forms.

The top of a mist pool is often flat. If you were to climb up through it, you could feel the air suddenly get warmer as you pass out of the mist into clear air.

Top: An orb-web spider like this builds a round web with spokes radiating from its center. The web is clearly visible in the mist.

Opposite: If the wind blows after sunrise, mist that formed in the valley bottom overnight can get blown back up the hillside.

Below: On a misty morning, thousands of spiders' webs appear, covered in tiny drops of water.

Salmon Leap

Salmon Leap

Top: Female Atlantic salmon change color from silver to purple when they are ready to lay eggs.

Below: Brown trout eggs hatch in late autumn. The newly hatched fish with their big yolk sacs stay along the gravel of the streambed.

The rain brought by autumn storms runs off the land and into streams and rivers. Instead of the clear trickles of cool water that flow in summer, many streams become cold, muddy torrents. This is good for salmon and trout that must swim up streams to reach the shallow, gravelly stretches where they lay their eggs. The cold temperature of the water helps the fish because cold water carries more oxygen than warm water. With plenty of oxygen, the fish have enough energy for their difficult journey upstream.

Atlantic salmon spend the summer resting in deep pools of water, far downriver. There, they wait for the first spate, or flood, of autumn. As river levels rise, and the water becomes muddy and cool, the fish begin to move upriver. The journey is easy at first. The water is deep, and the current is not strong. Farther upstream, the going becomes more difficult. There are rapids and waterfalls to conquer. The fish may have to wait weeks for more rain to deepen the waters. Only then can they swim up the rapids, keeping very close to the rocks to avoid the strongest currents.

Fish cannot swim up vertical waterfalls, although they will sometimes try. Getting past a waterfall is like a human running up an escalator.

Rather than swimming up waterfalls, salmon leap over them. Each fish has to judge its leap so that it lands head first in the fast-flowing water at the top of the falls. Some fish try many times before they successfully leap over a steep waterfall. Once they *do* succeed, they continue onward in their journey.

Below: Atlantic salmon lay their eggs in small streams. To reach their **spawning grounds**, they have to swim up rapids and leap over waterfalls.

19

Hide or Fly?

Top: A red admiral butterfly rests on a rotten apple and drinks the juice. The sweet juice gives the butterfly energy to renew its journey.

Insects are very active in the summer. With the cooler weather of autumn, however, they become sluggish. Then they are easy **prey** for birds and other insect-eaters.

Insects try to protect themselves from the oncoming cold of winter. As autumn approaches, strong fliers, such as dragonflies and butterflies, fly to regions where the climate is warmer.

Many red admiral butterflies that were born and bred in northern Europe fly south in September. Scientists do not understand how the butterflies know when to go or in which direction to fly. It is possible that rapidly decreasing day length is the trigger for southward **migration**.

During autumn, hundreds of red admirals can sometimes be seen flying low over the ground toward the south. They have a particular energy-saving flight that involves four or five quick flaps

Right: This silver-y moth is almost invisible among the fallen leaves in autumn. Before the cold temperatures arrive, the moth will fly south.

of the wings, followed by a short glide — repeated again and again. Every chance they get during their long journey, red admirals refuel with **nectar** or fruit juice.

Even more remarkable is the long southward migration of the monarch butterflies of North America. When temperatures drop during autumn, some monarchs fly all the way from Canada to the mountains of Mexico — a distance of more than 1,240 miles (2,000 km). Hundreds of thousands of monarchs will settle in specific tree groves to spend the winter.

Above: Monarch butterflies from throughout North America head for Mexico in autumn. They travel to just a few very special places in the mountains.

Right: The first frosts of autumn spell doom for many plants and animals. Here, a wasp and the flower it is on have been killed by frost.

Most insects either do not or cannot fly to warmer climates, so they have to find some way of surviving winter where they are. Each butterfly species has its own preferred way of spending the cold months of the year.

Brimstone butterflies in Europe feed on flowers during late summer and early autumn. Then suddenly they disappear, and no one really knows where they go. Brimstones probably hide in dense bushes or ivy. Peacock butterflies look for hollow

Right: Brimstone butterflies may search out dense clumps of ivy in autumn. There, they may spend five or six months waiting for the warm weather of spring.

trees during autumn in which to hibernate. Some find safety in sheds and under roofs.

Only a few butterfly species hibernate as adults. The adults of most species die in autumn. For instance, the white butterflies that are so common around cabbages in summer die out in autumn. Their caterpillars, however, search for sheltered spots where they change into **pupae**. The pupae of these butterflies hibernate.

In autumn, the tiny caterpillars of marsh fritillaries spin a dense web of silk among the lower stems of their food plant. There, they spend the winter months protected by the silken tents.

In Mediterranean climates (mild climates similar to those found in countries bordering the Mediterranean Sea), autumn brings the first rain after the long, hot summer. Plants burst into leaf, and moths emerge from their pupae to lay large numbers of eggs. The caterpillars that hatch from these eggs munch their way through the lush plants that grow during the cool, wet winter.

Above: The gray-green, black-spotted pupa of a large white butterfly remains immobile through autumn storms and winter snows.

Left: A few adult aphids are still alive on this oak twig in autumn but will soon die. Their closely packed eggs, stuck on the twig, will survive to hatch next spring.

Fly South, Fly North

Top: The arctic tern breeds in arctic regions. It migrates to southern Africa and South America in autumn.

Below: In October, flocks of redwings arrive in southern Europe from the north. Redwings fly at night, and the "seep" of their calls coming out of the darkness is a sure sign that winter is on its way.

Birds are much stronger flyers than insects, and many of them flee the oncoming winter. It is not the cold that affects them. It is the scarcity of food. Birds, such as swallows and swifts, that feed on flying insects have to leave their summer homes in autumn because their food disappears.

In the Northern Hemisphere, the autumn bird migration starts as early as August. In Europe, swifts and cuckoos are mostly well on their way to Africa by the end of September. As the insect-eaters depart southward, the berry-eaters and grass-eaters arrive in Europe from the north. Huge flocks of redwings and fieldfares move in from

Scandinavia to gorge themselves on fruits and berries. Flocks of geese also leave their breeding grounds in Iceland, northern Europe, and Canada in autumn. They fly south to spend the winter in warmer climates where the grass is not covered with snow.

There are fewer migrating birds in the Southern Hemisphere because the far southern areas of the planet are mostly covered with ocean waters. Antarctica is too cold at all times of the year for land birds. In Australia, many birds fly north in autumn to spend the winter in Indonesia. Some of these birds actually fly south, however, opposite the expected direction. Most of Australia is **arid**, and desert birds, such as budgerigars, fly south to places where rain has fallen so they can feed and breed. Birds that cannot fly must walk. Emus, which are big, flightless birds similar to ostriches, begin a long walk south in autumn.

Above: European swallows fly south in autumn, heading for Africa. They must feed during their journey. Over this lake in eastern Africa, there are plenty of insects for the swallows to eat.

Left: A flock of budgerigars flies south in autumn, along the western coast of Australia. The birds settle in areas where winter rains provide food.

The Mating Game

Top: A bull elk sounds his fearsome call.

Above: This red deer stag sends a roar echoing around the valleys in Scotland.

Below: Two fallow deer bucks crash their antlers together in a show of strength.

Most birds **mate** in spring and lay eggs soon after. Mammals are different. They have a long wait after mating before their young are born. This wait is called the **gestation period**. Big animals generally have longer gestation periods than small animals. Large deer, such as elk or red deer, have a gestation period of seven or eight months. In order for the female to give birth in early summer, which is the best time for young calves, the male and female must mate sometime in autumn. In early November, the forests and mountains ring to the sound of stags bellowing to each other. Each stag rounds up as many females as he can. Fights break out when one stag tries to steal females from another, and the stags' antlers crash together.

Left: Bank voles feed on berries and acorns in autumn to build up fat reserves in their bodies. Autumn fat helps voles survive winter when food is scarce.

Autumn in many parts of the world is a time when animals in the wild prepare for the difficult and dangerous time ahead. Some animals store food. Mice store nuts in hollow trees or in the ground. Squirrels and some birds bury acorns and other nuts here, there, and everywhere.

Our human ancestors also prepared for winter. They stored food in autumn to help them survive the winter. They had to defend their food stores against thieves, just as many animals fight off raiders that come into their territory.

After the mild and easy days of summer, autumn is a period of great activity and hard work for the natural world. Its creatures must get ready for the less bountiful months that will soon come.

Below: In autumn, pikas store leaves that will provide food during the cold winter months.

Activities:

Spore Prints and Jelly

Spore Prints

In autumn in many parts of Europe and North America, people collect and dry edible mushrooms. They eat them during the rest of the year. Mushrooms and toadstools are the fruiting bodies of fungi. They produce millions of spores. Each spore could grow into a new fungus.

To see how mushrooms spread their spores, you will need some sheets of paper (both light and dark in color), a kitchen knife, and a bag in which to collect some mushrooms. Collect several different kinds of mushrooms, choosing only those that are fully open. Don't choose the ones that are so old they are beginning to sag.

Do not eat mushrooms that you find in the wild. They could be highly poisonous. Wash your hands carefully after handling wild mushrooms because of the possibility of poison. If you cannot find wild mushrooms in your area, buy several different kinds of "open-cup" mushrooms at a supermarket near you.

Place some sheets of paper on a table in a quiet corner of the house. Weigh the paper down around the edges to avoid curling. Cut the stalks off the mushrooms as close as possible to the gills (ridges). Arrange them, gills down, on the sheets of paper *as shown above*. Put mushrooms with dark gills on white paper and mushrooms with white

gills on dark paper. Wait for about twenty-four hours for "spore prints" to form. The spores will fall out from between the gills and settle onto the paper in a pattern matching exactly the pattern of gills. The spores fall directly onto the paper because there is no breeze inside a house to scatter them. Next, carefully remove the mushrooms, trying not to damage the delicate prints beneath.

Fruit Jelly

Not many of the fruits of autumn will last through winter without special preparation. One way of preserving fruits is to turn them into jelly. Three things are needed for fruit jelly to set — sugar, acid, and pectin. Acid is found in most fruits. It is the substance that makes them taste sour. Pectin is a substance found in fruits that binds cell walls together.

To make fruit jelly, choose some sour fruit, such as cranberries or crab apples.

You will also need water, a large saucepan, a large spoon, a measuring cup, a large bowl, a muslin "jelly bag" (or a large handkerchief with some string tied firmly to its corners), sugar, measuring scales, and jelly jars. Ask an adult to help you make your first batch of jelly.

Wash the fruit, and put it into the saucepan. If you are using apples, cut them into slices first. Do not fill the saucepan more than halfway with fruit. Pour water into the pan until it almost covers the fruit. Some fruit, such as cranberries, may float. In that case, measure the volume of fruit in the measuring cup, and then add the same volume of water. Boil the fruit gently until it is soft and mushy. Then let it cool.

Next, suspend the jelly bag (or the handkerchief) over a large bowl. With a spoon, scoop the fruit into the bag. Allow the bag to drip overnight.

The next day, measure the amount of juice with the measuring cup and put it into a clean saucepan. For each 1/2 cup (120 milliliters) of juice, add 3 ounces (85 grams) of sugar. Bring the contents of the saucepan to a boil, stirring until all the sugar has dissolved. The jelly is hot, and it may boil over if you do not lower the heat soon enough. If the pan starts to fill with bubbles, slide it off the heat until the bubbles subside. Leave the pan on low heat so that the jelly gently simmers.

It is now time to test if the setting point has been reached. Put a teaspoonful of the hot liquid onto a cold, dry plate. Leave it for a few minutes. After this liquid cools, slide your finger over the surface of the plate and into the liquid. If your finger pushes up a wrinkly skin of fruit, the setting point has been reached, and you can put the jelly into jars. If the setting point for the jelly has not yet been reached, simmer it a little longer and perform the test again.

When the setting point has been reached, allow the liquid jelly to cool a little before scooping it out of the pan and into warm, dry, screw-topped jars. If the lids of your jelly jars fit properly and they are put on when the jelly is still hot, you can enjoy your preserved fruit jelly for years.

Glossary

annuals: plants that grow from seed, produce flowers, make seeds themselves, and then die — all in one year.

arid: dry.

axis: a line through the middle of an object around which the object turns.

capsules: small containers.

chlorophyll: the pigment that makes plants green.

condenses: changes from a vapor to a liquid (and sometimes to a solid).

day length: the time between sunrise and sunset.

equinox: the time of year when the Sun is directly over the Equator, and day and night are of equal length everywhere.

evaporate: to change from a liquid to a vapor.

flowering plants: the kinds of plants that produce flowers.

flowerless plants: the kinds of plants, such as mosses and ferns, that do not produce flowers.

fruiting bodies: the visible parts of fungi that produce spores.

genes: the very complex molecules that determine which characteristics are passed on from one generation to the next. There are thousands of genes in a cell, and every cell in an animal or plant contains the same set of genes.

gestation period: the period between mating and the birth of young.

hemisphere: one-half of Earth, divided at the Equator.

hibernate: to spend winter at rest.

mate: when a male and female join together to produce offspring.

migration: the movement of animals from one place to another.

molecules: the smallest parts of a substance, made up of two or more atoms that are joined.

mycelia: the usually hidden parts of fungi consisting of fine threads.

nectar: the sweet liquid produced by flowers to attract bees, birds, and other animals.

orbit: a circular or oval path taken by a heavenly body, such as Earth.

perennials: plants that normally live for more than two years.

prey: creatures that are hunted by other creatures for food.

pupae: the stage in the development of insects before they become adults.

spawning grounds: areas where aquatic animals deposit their eggs.

species: a distinct kind of animal or plant that produces offspring with another member of its specific group.

spores: microscopic grains produced by flowerless plants and fungi from which new plants grow.

vapor: a gas formed from a liquid.

Plants and Animals

The common names of plants and animals vary from language to language. Their scientific names, based on Greek or Latin words, are the same the world over. Each kind of plant or animal has two scientific names. The first name is called the genus. It starts with a capital letter. The second name is the species name. It starts with a small letter.

arctic tern *(Sterna paradisaea)* — worldwide 24

aspen *(Populus tremuloides)* — North America 7

Atlantic salmon *(Salmo salar)* — North America, Iceland, Greenland, Europe 18, 19

beech *(Fagus sylvatica)* — Europe, planted in North America 7, 15

dandelion *(Taraxacum officinale)* — Europe, introduced elsewhere 8, 9

elk *(Cervus canadensis)* — North America 26

Engelmann prickly pear cactus *(Opuntia engelmannii)* — Americas, introduced elsewhere 10

fallow deer *(Dama dama)* — southern Europe, introduced elsewhere 26

hair moss *(Polytrichum commune)* — Europe 12

holly *(Ilex aquifolium)* — Europe, western Asia; planted in North America 11

horse chestnut *(Aesculus hippocastanum)* — northern Greece, Albania; planted in Europe, North America 9

Korean mountain ash *(Sorbus alnifolia)* — eastern Asia 10

large white butterfly *(Pieris brassicae)* — Europe, Asia 23

monarch butterfly *(Danaus plexippus)* — North America 21

pika *(Ochotona princeps)* — North America 27

red deer *(Cervus elaphus)* — northern Europe 26

redwing *(Turdus iliacus)* — northern Europe and Asia 11, 24

roe deer *(Capreolus capreolus)* — Europe 4, 5

silver-y moth *(Plusia gamma)* — North America, Europe, northern Africa 20

subalpine fir *(Abies lasiocarpa)* — North America 16

Books to Read

Animals in the Fall (Preparing for Winter). Gail Saunders-Smith (Pebble Books)

Autumn Science Projects. (Seasonal Science Projects series). John Williams (Julian Messner)

How Animals Protect Themselves. Animal Survival (series). Michel Barré (Gareth Stevens)

The Nature and Science of Leaves. Exploring the Science of Nature (series). Jane Burton and Kim Taylor (Gareth Stevens)

Weather. Young Scientist Concepts and Projects (series). Robin Kerrod (Gareth Stevens)

Why Do We Have Different Seasons? Ask Isaac Asimov (series). (Gareth Stevens)

Videos and Web Sites

Videos

Birds and Migration. (International Film Bureau)
Deciduous Forest. (Coronet)
Flowers, Plants, and Trees. (Library Video)
Insects. (TMW Media)
Learning About Leaves. (Encyclopædia Britannica Educational Corporation)
Look. A Butterfly. (Bullfrog)

Web Sites

www.esf.edu/pubprog/brochure/leaves/leaves.htm
www.worldbook.com/fun/seasons/html/seasons.htm
www.whitemtn.org/autumn.html
bellnetweb.brc.tamus.edu/res_grid/elementry/animtrks
www.arborday.net/kids/kid_links.htm

Some web sites stay current longer than others. For further web sites, use your search engines to locate the following topics: *animal survival, autumn, chlorophyll, leaves,* and *migration.*

Index